# Elements of Design

# COLOR AND VALUE

# Elements of Design

# COLOR
# and VALUE

**Joseph A. Gatto**

*Art Teacher*
Los Angeles, California

Distributed by
STERLING PUBLISHING CO., INC.
419 Park Avenue South
New York, N. Y. 10016

DAVIS PUBLICATIONS, INC.
Worcester, Massachusetts

*To my mother, Ben*
*and Nicole*

Printed in the United States of America
Library of Congress Catalog Card Number:
ISBN 0-87192-065-4

*Printing:* Davis Press
*Type:* 10 point Theme Medium
*Graphic Design:* Thumbnail Associates

*Consulting Editors:* Gerald F. Brommer, George F. Horn, Sarita R. Rainey

10  9  8  7  6  5  4  3  2  1

All photographs by the author, unless otherwise noted.

# CONTENTS

# Color Effects Visual Communication

Every day you see signs while walking or riding along streets —
often wondering why some are more recognizable than others.
Color makes visual communication more effective. Photo
courtesy Volkswagen of America.

# WHAT COLOR DOES

Close your eyes for a few minutes. Try to visualize yourself in a world without color — without color to expressively interpret your environment.

As you open your eyes, you suddenly realize that the possibilities of color are wonderful, interesting and unlimited. Color makes life enjoyable and provides you with many exciting pleasures. Color makes dressing up fun; renders your home restful or exciting; the foods you eat, more enjoyable; and your possessions, more personal.

Color is constantly changing with the forces of nature, providing you with unlimited variations to study and enjoy. It is possible there are many unique colors in your immediate area waiting to be discovered: rusted signs, neon lights, oil spill from a parked car, your back pack and countless other objects you see or pass every day.

The next time you are in a familiar spot, observe how many colors you have passed unknowingly — perhaps a rack of clothing at the dry cleaners, the multicolored fruits and vegetables at the supermarket, or the birds and fish at the pet store. Examine color more closely and explore your exciting discoveries about it and what it does.

## Color Reinforces Written Words

Safety devices and warnings are reinforced by the use of color.

The blinking of the red light (red traditionally means danger) is an alert to stop — do not cross the street.

The artist Picasso used color and value to record the events of Guernica. Color was also used to emphasize our achievements in space and to record the attempts to save a beautiful city.

# Color Records Events

# Color Designates And Identifies

The windsock, a simple form of contrasting color, designates wind conditions to aid the pilot in a safe landing.

Resistors, transistors with circuit boards consisting of colored wires — yellow to green, orange to blue provide easy identification for assembling and repairing.

# Color Establishes Moods

How many times have you felt blue? Color has the ability to
establish moods. When dark colors dominate art work, moods
of gloom, mystery or drama are created, while light colors
have the opposite effect. Often the emotional feeling comes
through intuition and not from intellectual reasoning. This
ability of color to create moods also serves as the vehicle for
expressing personal emotions and feelings. Selective use of
dark colors also creates a feeling of space when seen next to
contrasting colors.

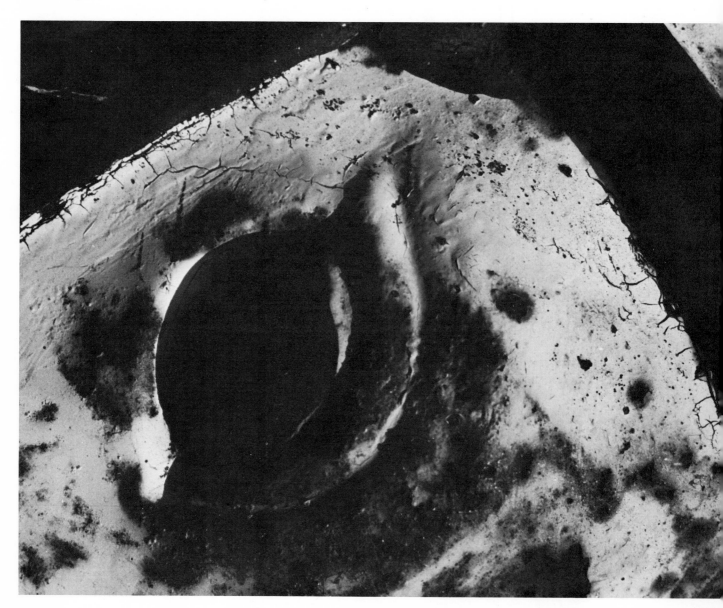

This popular soft drink relies on color to achieve instant recognition as an aid in selling. The colors are red, green and white.

The colors you like are changed from time to time. The manufacturers of the products invest vast sums of money attempting to determine your color preferences because color is a major marketing factor.

# Color Sells Products

Red, orange and yellow are visually strong colors. The red flag at the back of the truck warns following vehicles of the danger of an overhanging object.

The surrounding areas near the telephone are green. Use of a red shell enables the telephone to be seen more easily and to attract attention.

Why are fireboxes red? Red is a vibrant color and quickly attracts attention.

# Color Attracts Attention

## Color Symbolizes

Color has the ability to signify different meanings as the red, white and blue of the flag painted on this wall. Colors represent symbols, ideas and personal emotions. Compare the symbolism of red, white and blue with other objects of similar colors.

Red for blood, white for bandages, and blue added for loyalty have long been symbolic colors of the barber. Early barbers not only cut hair but also rendered first aid and medication.

# Color Decorates

Do colors have sounds? Do sounds have colors? This fine old
mandolin was decorated with colored woods and pigment.

# Color Expresses Feelings

Color aids in the expression of personal emotions and feelings.
Designing, making and wearing unique clothing allow young
people to find new ways of expression, along with the
traditional forms such as painting and drawing.

We enjoy pleasant drives or walks on our streets. Visual pollution is a serious concern. Color enriches the environment and makes our cities more attractive.

# Color Creates Environments

Your immediate environment lends opportunities of experimenting with color. Through the selective use of color, you can create surroundings that will provide many different moods in your home.

Look at the meeting of two contrasting colors on the handle of the blow-off valve and the shadow cast by the rod. The meeting point of two contrasting colors on a two-dimensional surface creates line.

# CHARACTERISTICS OF COLOR

It is difficult to determine when and how color was first used by man. In early civilizations man recognized that light — sunlight — was essential to life. Color, as a manifestation of light, held important meaning to man by allowing him to interpret the very core of physical reality.

Most people become aware of and react to color at an early stage in life. Our environment — natural and man-made — contributed to our understanding of color.

Knowledge of color was increased by the work of the physiologist, the chemist, the physicist, the psychologist and the artist. The knowledge gained and applied within the framework of the art elements contributed to the enrichment of life and to an increased understanding of art.

Contrasting colors are everywhere. Note the lines created by contrasting colors on the lettering, vents and on the fenders of the fire truck. Basically, lines are curved, straight, or bent.

## Color And Line

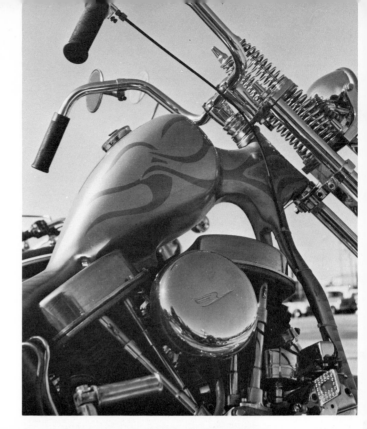

The forms seen every day are made more personal with the addition of color. How many forms can you see around you that have been enriched by color?

By the use of color, the form of a functional instrument such as the telephone is emphasized. Color can be form.

# Color And Form

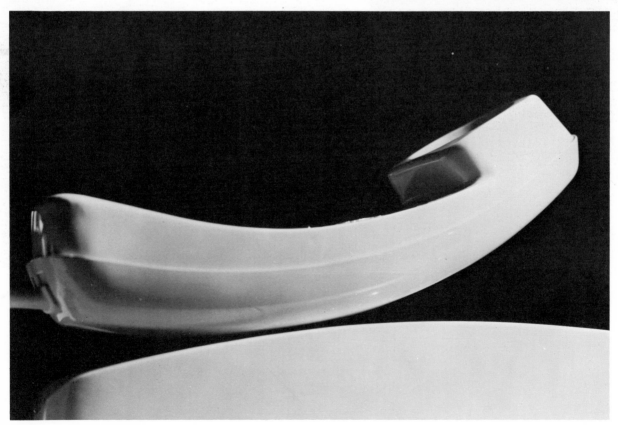

# Color And Space

It is possible to give paintings the illusion of space by the
placement of color and to create interest through the balance
of backward and forward movement of color.
Color is used to give depth to a pictorial surface.

## Color And Value

Exposure to sun, wind and rain caused the colors to lose their brightness. Now they reflect subtle variations of value. Value may supplement or even replace color as on this old house.

# Color And Texture

One of the most important properties of color is its ability to produce texture (that part of a surface to which our sense of touch responds), like the dried material on this telephone pole. Similar surfaces can be created by student artists using color.

Three-dimensional forms in color when reproduced on two-dimensional surfaces (such as paintings, drawings or photography), can create visual texture. The produced textures are called visual textures because they can be seen.

Color is used by a variety of people for different reasons. As you learn more about color and its problems, you will be able to apply this knowledge to a variety of situations. Color is used in new and creative ways every day by a number of industries and services — manufacturing and packaging, communications and safety, decorative and recreational to name just a few.

An environment that includes color is necessary to the development of children because the presence of color contributes considerably to their mental and physical growth.

# PRACTICAL USES OF COLOR

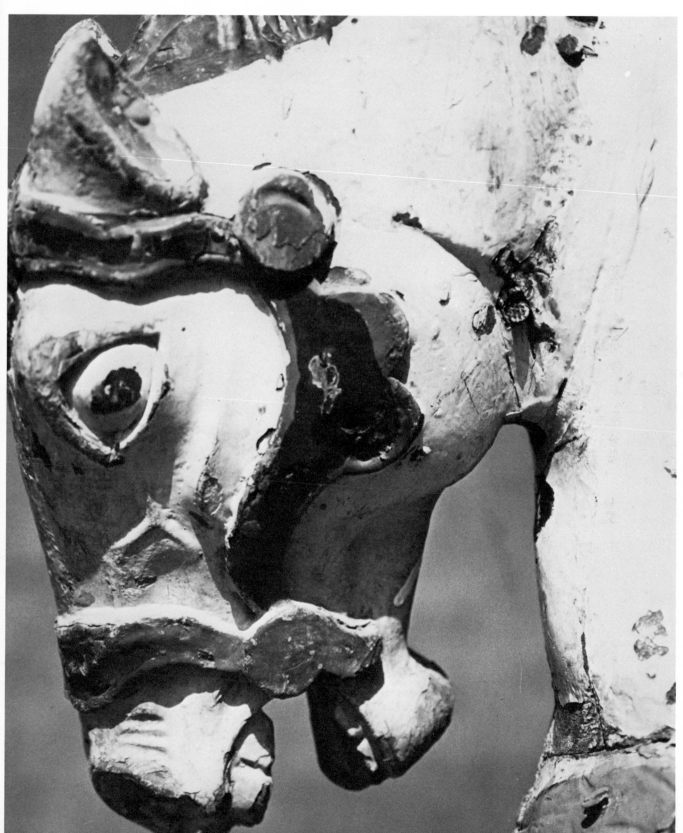

# Use By Artists And Collectors

For thousands of years, artists have used color to communicate their ideas. In the past pigments were made of root dyes, earth colors and animal fat and applied by various art techniques. Chemically produced pigments and the brush often meet the needs of today's young artists.

As part of the small African sculpture, multicolored beads were sewn on to serve as a decorative element. The primitive sculptor saw color differently from the contemporary art collector.

26

# Use By Environmentalists And Educators

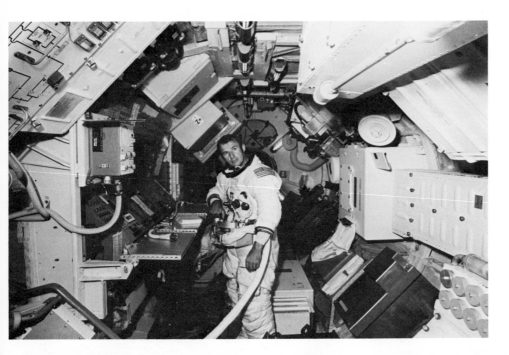

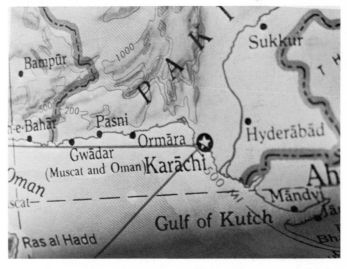

Our space explorers are trained to react to color with split-second accuracy.

Just as color provides for the needs of man on earth, future space expeditions must provide for the habitability of man. Color is a vital factor and will accommodate the explorers on their long journeys. Photos courtesy NASA.

Color has always aided the educator in the clarification of important facts necessary to acquiring knowledge. Maps in color help define the geography of man.

# Use By Scientists

The tripod-like object is a gnomon and a photometric chart assembly. It is used as a photographic reference to establish lunar color. Photo courtesy NASA.

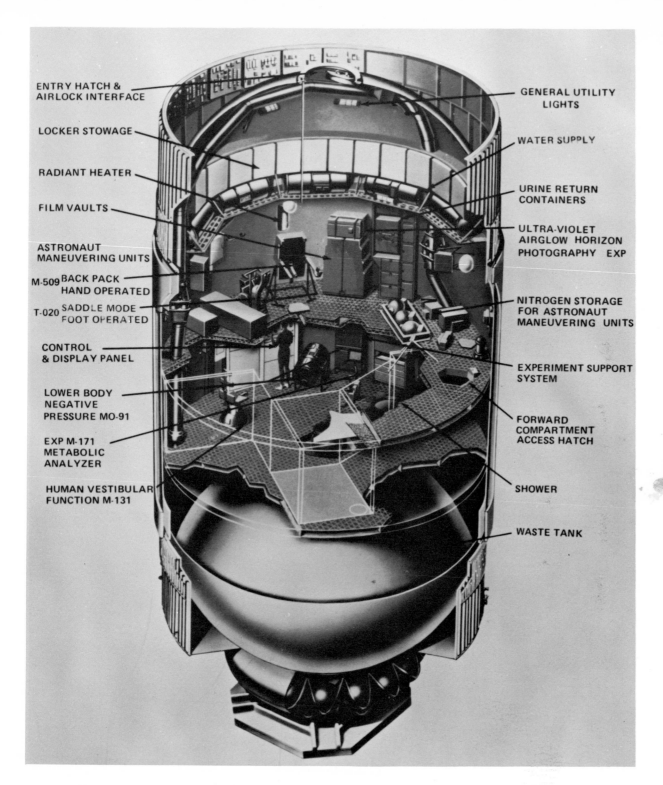

ENTRY HATCH &
AIRLOCK INTERFACE

LOCKER STOWAGE

RADIANT HEATER

FILM VAULTS

ASTRONAUT
MANEUVERING UNITS

M-509 BACK PACK
HAND OPERATED

T-020 SADDLE MODE
FOOT OPERATED

CONTROL
& DISPLAY PANEL

LOWER BODY
NEGATIVE
PRESSURE MO-91

EXP M-171
METABOLIC
ANALYZER

HUMAN VESTIBULAR
FUNCTION M-131

GENERAL UTILITY
LIGHTS

WATER SUPPLY

URINE RETURN
CONTAINERS

ULTRA-VIOLET
AIRGLOW HORIZON
PHOTOGRAPHY EXP

NITROGEN STORAGE
FOR ASTRONAUT
MANEUVERING UNITS

EXPERIMENT SUPPORT
SYSTEM

FORWARD
COMPARTMENT
ACCESS HATCH

SHOWER

WASTE TANK

# Use By Illustrators

Illustrators use color to demonstrate important facts often not possible with photography, such as this cutaway view of skylab. Photo courtesy NASA.

29

## Use By Entertainment Industry

Centers of entertainment, such as amusement parks, theaters and restaurants, provide additional moods of drama, excitement or relaxation through the use of color.

## Use In Sports And By Auto Stylists

Color is vital to many aspects of professional sports: uniforms, pennants and tickets. Tickets printed in color designate the location of your seat. Even parking areas and landscaping contribute to the "color" of the home team.

Color is an important element to the individuality of the old show car.

Recent developments in materials have offered the architect new freedom in building design. The all-glass facade reflects the many colors of the landscape, parking area and reflecting pools below as well as the changing seasons. In a true sense, the building creates its own color environment.

The purpose of any advertisement is to attract attention and to communicate as much as possible about what is being advertised. The advertisement for a popular soft drink uses color, line and form in a highly creative and harmonious manner. Photo courtesy 7-Up Company, St. Louis, Mo.

# Color And Advertisers And Architects

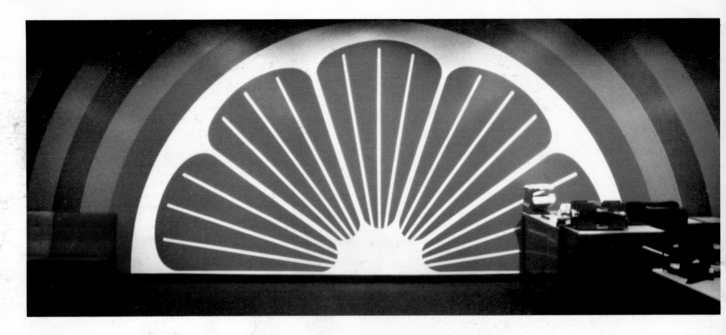

# Use By Interior Designers And Sculptors

Color is frequently used to enhance the working environment. Color helps prevent boredom, increases productivity and reduces accidents. Photography Wayne Thom, courtesy Albert C. Martin and Associates.

This sculpture combines the traditional concepts of describing form by light and dark values. Color adds additional excitement. Photo courtesy Ralph Bacerra, Sculptor.

34

Breathtaking colors for us to choose from! The many
ingredients have unique properties individually, but when
combined, create exciting colors, textures, tastes and smells
for your enjoyment. Photography Glen Embree, courtesy,
Baskin-Robbins Ice Cream.

# Use By Industrial Designers

Rich woods, appealing designs and excellent craftsmanship contribute to beautiful furniture. Color further enhances the furniture. Photo courtesy of Designer-Craftsman Sam Maloof.

The comfort of the passenger is paramount to the airlines. Warm, restful colors are often used in the lounge of large jet liners. Correctly selected colors provide a relaxed atmosphere for the passenger and tend to reduce strain from long journeys and relieve boredom. Photography Wayne Thom, courtesy Albert C. Martin and Associates.

Civic pride and a desire to enhance the environment led to the painting of the parkway. The harmonious color delights people on foot and creates excitement for airline passengers. Gene Davis' Franklin's Footpath, courtesy Philadelphia Museum of Art.

# COLOR WHEEL

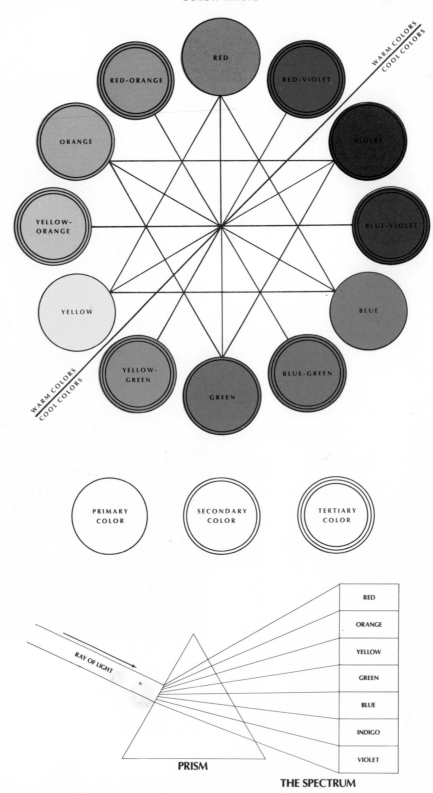

RED

RED-ORANGE

RED-VIOLET

WARM COLORS
COOL COLORS

ORANGE

VIOLET

YELLOW-
ORANGE

BLUE-VIOLET

YELLOW

BLUE

YELLOW-
GREEN

BLUE-GREEN

WARM COLORS
COOL COLORS

GREEN

PRIMARY
COLOR

SECONDARY
COLOR

TERTIARY
COLOR

RAY OF LIGHT

| RED |
|-----|
| ORANGE |
| YELLOW |
| GREEN |
| BLUE |
| INDIGO |
| VIOLET |

PRISM

THE SPECTRUM

38

# PROPERTIES OF COLOR

Color is an exciting part of our world. It is all around us; we see it everywhere we look. Color is an element of art that appeals directly to our emotions and is universal in appreciation. It has instant appeal to the small child, as well as the adult.

We see color that is sometimes bright, sometimes dull; exciting and interesting; harmonious or chaotic. We cross streets filled with color, make purchases because of color, eat, sleep and drink color. Some colors cause us to cheer, shout and scream (like our school colors). Other colors make us cry, feel happy or depressed.

Great nations have defended their colors; vast economies are dependent on color. It is below us, above us and completely immerses us at times. It is here for us to learn about and enjoy.

Color begins with and is derived from light — either natural or artificial. We see the sensation of color because we respond to different wavelengths of light. We can see the effects of a beam of light as it passes through a prism. The rays of light are bent or refracted as they pass through the glass at different angles and are seen as different colors. Our sense of vision interprets these colors which we call a spectrum.

To make the study of color easier, the spectrum is arranged in a circle. Spectrum colors are pure and bright, while the coloring matter or pigments that the artist uses are not as strong. It is important to remember that pigments cannot hope to duplicate the brightness of spectrum colors of light.

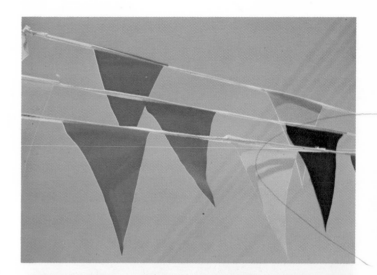

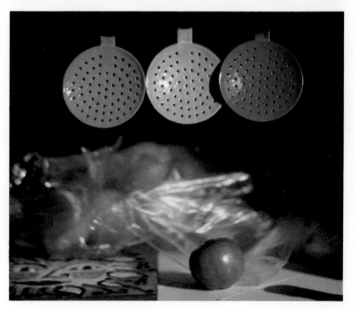

Red, yellow and blue are primary colors. The primary colors are theoretically the basis for the mixture of all colors. When any two of the three primary colors are mixed, the result is called a secondary color. Another name for color is hue.

Orange, green and violet are secondary colors. Note their use on the kitchen utensils to enhance food preparation.

## Primary And Secondary Colors

# Analogous Colors

Analogous colors share similar colors and are compatible when mixed together: red and orange, orange and yellow, blue and green.

## Warm Colors

The colors on this van are warm. They are so called because they are psychologically and symbolically associated with warm things. Warm colors make forms appear larger.

Unlike warm colors, cool colors — being at the opposite end of the spectrum — are less visible. Blues, greens and some violets are cool and are associated with sky, air and water. When cool colors are used in art work, forms may look smaller and suggest the illusion of space on the pictorial surface.

## Cool Colors

41

# Intensity Of Color

The colors in the rug beater are of low intensity. Intensity also refers to the purity of color. In this way it differs from *value* which refers to the quality of light which a color reflects. Value is concerned with light whereas intensity is concerned with color.

The colors in the god's eye, made of yarn, are very bright. The brightness or dullness of color, its strength or weakness, is called intensity or chroma. Intensity is the absence of any visible admixture of color.

# Complementary Colors

Nature is continually providing color harmonies for us to enjoy. Flowers and leaves, trees and fruit, animals and birds are good examples. The red tomatoes and green peppers provide a dramatic example of complementary color harmony.

Complementary colors are opposites. They are opposite each other on the color wheel. The designer of the stained-glass window in a contemporary church has incorporated all the complementary harmonies in one panel. Included are red and green, blue and orange, yellow and violet.

# Monochromatic Colors

It is possible to produce interesting results by using only one color and mixing it with neutrals (black and white) to achieve tints, tones and shades of that color.

# Bright And Dull Colors

One of the characteristics of color is its brightness or dullness, which is determined by the amount of light reflected from the surface. The colors on the Japanese kite appear brighter because of the strong sunlight filtering through the paper.

Water and lack of sunlight cause the dull-colored fish to appear even duller and the other fish to appear dull, even though the markings are quite vivid.

Many times we see both brightness and dullness. The dull coloring of the ceramic birdbath and the bright flower offer the opportunity for instant comparison of color, brightness and dullness.

# Color And Values

Light determines the value of a color. The apples facing the sun appear lighter. Because the paper under the apples receives less light, it appears darker in value than that of the paper in the plate.

Bent metal receives light differently and will create value changes on the surface. The metal closest to the light source seems lighter, and the metal away from the light appears darker, almost black. If you add white to a color, it will become lighter in value. If black or a darker color is added, the color gets lower in value.

# Neutral Colors

All things seen do not necessarily have color as we know it.
Some objects are black, white or gray and are called neutrals
because any one color is not distinguishable. Neutrals do not
look like any colors of the spectrum. They differ in the
amount of light which is reflected from them.

# The Effect Of Light

Color is dependent on the type of light and on the time of day. The beach umbrella seen in full sunlight demonstrates the vividness of color. The clearness of sunlight causes the edges of forms and details to be more evident. Colors and forms are seen more clearly in full sunlight.

Artificial light contributes to the way color is seen. The many values of colors in the fish market are subtle and muted because of the weak tungsten light source. Other artificial light sources are neon lights and fluorescent tubes, many of which distort the true color of objects.

# FACTORS AFFECTING COLOR

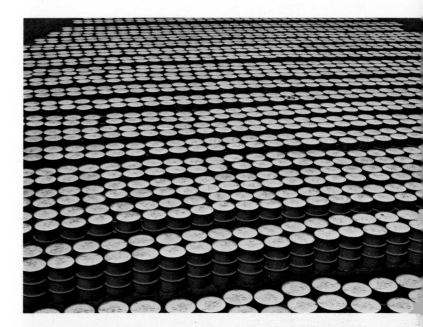

The more you know about color, the more you will be able to appreciate the factors that change color. Your eye color may vary under certain light conditions. A day at the beach can darken your skin but lighten your hair or fade the color of your blanket. In addition to the changes constantly effected by the natural elements, man also affects color.

What makes color interesting and exciting is your being receptive to the changes it goes through, recognizing why it changes and then appreciating the infinite variations possible.

Colors that normally seem to advance optically (as warmer colors do) are changed by distance. Color is also influenced by the curvature of the earth and the increased atmosphere. The red diminishes in intensity as the distance increases and the light gets weaker.

The color on the hanging lamps becomes darker in value because the distance from the observer increases. Detail in the color is lost and forms seem to blend together because of the loss of contrast.

# Color And The Season

Color changes with the seasons. In autumn, the warmer colors are seen; and in winter, cooler colors seem to dominate.

Seasonal color influences our immediate environment. On this rainy, winter day, the colors are lower in value because the intensity of light is reduced by atmospheric conditions.

# Mixing Color

Colors placed on top of other colors or very near to each other will create an optical mixture. The orange rust has influenced the adjacent colors and, in the case of the blue, has grayed it down because complementary colors mixed together produce gray. Our eyes can mix colors.

# Color And The Emotions
## (Excitement Of Color)

Color is all around us in the environment — natural and man made. We see color that is sometimes bright, sometimes dull, exciting and interesting, sometimes harmonious with the environment, sometimes chaotic, natural or artificial; and though we are not always aware of it, it makes a lasting impression on us. Our primary reaction to form is based on color, affecting our emotions directly and immediately. The more we know about color, the more we will be able to see, recognize, use and appreciate color.

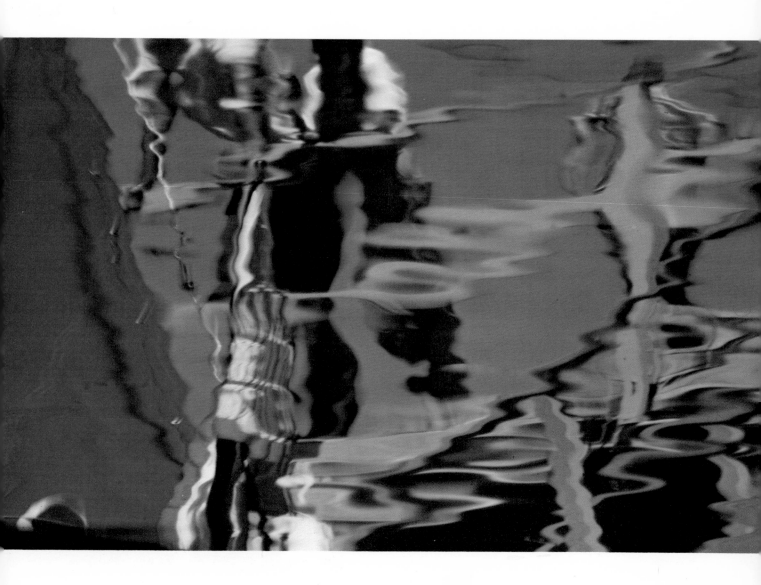

In order to understand art more fully, the relationship of value to the other art elements, such as form and space, must be considered. All of these elements; i.e., color, line, texture, form and space, must demonstrate some value contrast with the material with which you are working in order to remain visible. Line placement will produce value. Shapes are distinguished from each other by the use of value. Reproduction of textures relies on values in the shadows and highlights, and the very existence of color is dependent on value.

The spotlight, even though chromed, appears dark as well as light, because the highly polished exterior reflects different nearby surfaces creating value variation.

# CHARACTERISTICS OF VALUE

Value is the lightness and darkness of color. The fenders of the old sports car, as well as other parts of the automobile's body, receive different amounts of light, depending on the position of the car to the sunlight, and appear to be darker.

# Value Contrasts

Do you see the value changes in the plates of food, the bottle, the rich wood and the wrapped gift?

Values are created when the sun is quite bright and objects are at angles to it. The wire rolls create strong value contrasts of light color against the dark shadow areas. Detail lost in the core of the wire is due to the darkness of the value. This produces the suggestion of depth.

# Tints, Tones, Shades And Shadows

Strong sun on the sea gull has added to the value differences. In addition to the natural values, other values are created by the lack of light underneath the body, legs and feet. There is also a cast shadow from the beak creating a darker value on the breast of the bird. Dark areas of value are called shades; middle values are called tones; and light values are referred to as tints.

# Shadows and Highlights

Sunlight is a direct cause of value and will make objects appear lighter in value. On the other hand, when objects (for example, white canvas) are shaded from the sun, they appear dark. Value is the amount of lightness and darkness in black, white and gray. Color can be emphasized by the darker values of shadows.

# Range Of Values

There is an unlimited range of values that can be created, depending on the media used. Values can range from black to white as the values in the trees, grass and sky.

The sewing box edge and positions of the spools have cast shadows resulting in the darkened values of the thread.

Value can be subtle as on the medicine bottles or bold as in the dandelions and contrasting shrubs.

# Effect Of Sunlight And Shadows

Direct sunlight on the pulleys makes some areas very light, forcing loss of detail. Strong light-dark contrasts allow sharp focus because of strong illumination. Near objects are seen more easily. Distant objects are less bright and tend to be less distinct.

# FACTORS AFFECTING VALUE

Objects cannot receive light from all directions at one time. A solid object will receive more light from one side than another because that side is closer to the light source. Light will vary according to the surface of the object receiving the light. A round surface will have an even flow of light and dark, while angular surfaces will show sudden contrast. Cast shadows will also influence the value of an object.

The eaves of the feed store and the late afternoon sun create shaded areas on the wall. The shadows cast from the chicken feeders demonstrate the value changes created by shaded areas.

The cast shadow on the screen door and door jamb produces a darker value. Detail on the surface is reduced, while areas in full sunlight produce the opposite effect. Shaded areas will cause forms and details to darken. Details will virtually disappear. Artists use shaded areas to suggest the illusion of space.

61

Another source of value is artificial light. Tungsten light, fluorescent light and neon lights all produce different values. Compare forms in sunlight with forms in artificial light.

Ordinary surfaces allow us to observe different qualities of value. Compare the surfaces that reflect light with those that absorb light and with those that have translucent surfaces. Also compare areas that are not affected by direct sunlight.

# Effect Of Artificial Light And Surface Changes

# Effect Of Surface Changes On Value Patterns

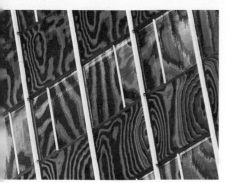

Different surface textures enable the comparison of values. The variety of textures in the junk-yard still life allows us to observe the subtle values on metal, cloth, rope, wood and paper.

Value patterns are created on windows that show stresses from building weight, heat, cold and wind. The value patterns are also influenced by the position of the viewer in relationship to the windows.

Variable surfaces will create different values. The wooden crates holding the large water bottles are used and worn; their values will appear different from the newly cut and stacked lumber.

# Value Describes Form

The floaters used by fishermen demonstrate how value describes roundness of form. The values are from light to dark. Darker value is observed on those floaters shaded from the sun.

# WHAT VALUE DOES

Value, like color, has wide application. An understanding of the art elements contributes to the appreciation of what value does.

In your art work, you can give roundness to forms, create the illusion of depth, reproduce textures and give the feeling of movement on the pictorial surface through the application of value. Our perception of objects is affected primarily by the distribution of light and dark on their surfaces and the correct placement of value will describe form on a two-dimensional surface.

The shadow pattern on the flower bud demonstrates how value becomes darker as the form moves away from the observer and gets lighter as the form comes forward. The transition is very subtle. Light and dark values show the roundness of form.

# Value Creates Centers OF Interest

Strong value and color contrast create interest and are important when trying to show a center of interest on a pictorial surface. The strong contrasting values draw the viewer's attention to the flowers in the window.

Abstract textures can be seen in the detail of the torn posters. Furthermore, the value contrast of the torn posters creates strong diagonal lines causing considerable visual activity on the pictorial surface. The artist can use values indicating textures for compositional purposes, such as variety, accent or emphasis. Contrasting values (chairs and lettering from the torn posters) attract attention.

The contrasting black handle against the white garage door attracts attention by value contrast.

# Value Defines Space

Values on the gate contrasting with the values in the background create the illusion of space. The darker the background values get, the greater the illusion of space appears on the pictorial surface.

Lack of contrast in the water and in the tiles of the water fountain demonstrate the illusion of shallow space. The knowledge of creating shallow, as well as deep, space is equally important to the young artist.

# Visual Communication

Value is necessary to visual communication, especially when it
involves saying something important to someone important.

# PRACTICAL USES OF VALUE

One of the most generally useful applications of value is in the description of objects, shapes and space. The descriptive qualities can include the psychological, the emotional and the expressive.

Faded inks, glare from the sun, weathering and distance — all contribute to reduced value contrast and poor legibility of writing and lettering. Value contrast is necessary to the communication of your ideas.

# Communication And Graphic Design

Value contrast among the sign, lamp post and lettering must
be evident during daylight hours and, if necessary, at night.
Contrast of value must be considered by city planners to aid in
sign location and readability of lettering.

Contrast of value allows the easy readability of numbers and
lettering. Easy legibility enables identification even at a
distance, as on this train cabin.

This coin store is a good place to see value that is created by merging elements; for example, when a number of lines are placed alongside each other or when they cross each other as on this Civil War fifty dollar bill.

# Use By Architects

Architects use new materials, including tinted glass, and new building techniques to create beautiful buildings. Value changes are used intentionally to execute successful design. Photo courtesy Federal Reserve Bank of Minneapolis.

Architects consider the interest created by light and dark values in buildings and the values created by sunlight and artificial light. Value contrasts make buildings more visually stimulating and more enjoyable as far as working environments are concerned.

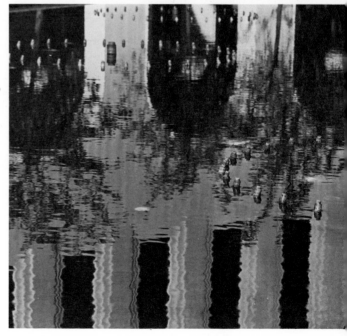

72

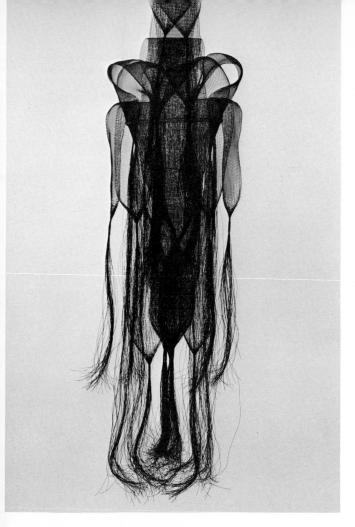

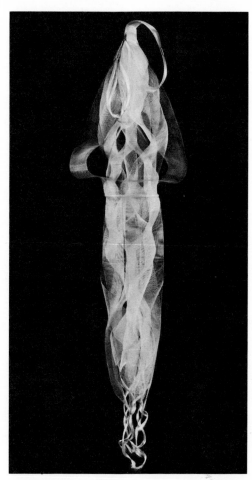

# Use By Craftsmen

Monofilament nylon was used to create exciting light and dark variations in the two weavings. *(Katsura* (left), *Amiyose III* (right), Photos by Stone and Steccati, courtesy Kay Sekimachi, Weaver.

Fabric designers create interesting value patterns in this applique design.

# Use By Artists

When drawing or painting, some artists use value instead of color, as it allows them to experiment with value without being overly concerned with color. (Rico Lebrun, *Crucifixion after Gruenwald*, Collection of the Author)

# Use By Industrial Designers

From gas station pumps to upholstery benches, value is an important factor for industrial designers to consider in marketing products and services.

# Use By Sculptors And Photographers

The sculptor must consider value important since it describes form. Traditionally, sculptors used value to create form which is pleasing and functional from many points of view. Such a consideration dictated that the near parts of the old tombstone marker be lighter and that the distant parts be darker.

Photographic composition will be aided considerably with correct use of value. Value is an important factor to the photographer in the execution of ideas, moods and emotions.

# INDEX

Production of this book was aided by the combined efforts of craftsmen, photographers and other interested people. My sincere thanks to Ralph Bacerra, Sculptor; Sam Maloof, Designer-Craftsman; Kay Sekimachi, Weaver; Photographers Stone and Steccati. Their assistance in furnishing excellent photographs of fine work was most helpful.

Also deep appreciation goes to the following people and to their companies for allowing me to use some of their published photographs in this book: Marilyn Slack, Public Relations, and Glen Embree, Photography, Baskin-Robbins Ice Cream Company; Charlaine Hobson, Public Information, Federal Reserve Bank of Minneapolis; Red Patterson, Vice President, Public Relations and Promotions, Los Angeles Dodgers; Bob Wilkerson, Albert C. Martin and Associates; Wayne Thom, Photography, also of Albert C. Martin and Associates; John McLeaish and C. C. Johnson, NASA; Sandra Horrocks, Manager, Public Relations, Philadelphia Museum of Art; Patricia Harden, Sunkist Growers, Inc.; Richard C. Carney, The 7-Up Company; Pattie Cota, Volkswagen of America.

My special thanks to my wife, Isolde, for editing and helping with the manuscript.

253

253